EMMANUEL JOSEPH

The Mind of the Market, Emotional Intelligence, Cultural Trends, and the Philosophy of Entrepreneurship

Copyright © 2025 by Emmanuel Joseph

All rights reserved. No part of this publication may be reproduced, stored or transmitted in any form or by any means, electronic, mechanical, photocopying, recording, scanning, or otherwise without written permission from the publisher. It is illegal to copy this book, post it to a website, or distribute it by any other means without permission.

First edition

This book was professionally typeset on Reedsy.
Find out more at reedsy.com

Contents

1	Chapter 1: The Essence of Emotional Intelligence	1
2	Chapter 2: The Role of Cultural Trends in Entrepreneurship	3
3	Chapter 3: The Philosophy of Entrepreneurship	5
4	Chapter 4: Emotional Intelligence in Leadership	7
5	Chapter 5: Adapting to Cultural Trends	9
6	Chapter 6: Innovation and Creativity	10
7	Chapter 7: Building a Strong Brand	11
8	Chapter 8: The Power of Networking	12
9	Chapter 9: Financial Management	13
10	Chapter 10: Marketing Strategies	15
11	Chapter 11: Customer Relationship Management	17
12	Chapter 12: Scaling Your Business	19
13	Chapter 13: Navigating Challenges and Setbacks	21
14	Chapter 14: Ethical Entrepreneurship	23
15	Chapter 15: The Future of Entrepreneurship	24
16	Chapter 16: The Entrepreneurial Mindset	26
17	Chapter 17: The Legacy of Entrepreneurship	27

1

Chapter 1: The Essence of Emotional Intelligence

Emotional Intelligence (EI) is the ability to understand and manage your own emotions and those of others. This skill is crucial for entrepreneurial success, as it helps in building relationships, resolving conflicts, and making informed decisions. Unlike traditional intelligence, EI involves empathy, self-awareness, and social skills, which are essential for navigating the complex world of business.

Understanding EI begins with self-awareness. Entrepreneurs must recognize their emotional triggers and responses to various situations. This awareness allows for better control over reactions, leading to more rational decision-making. Self-regulation, another component of EI, involves managing emotions in a healthy way, such as staying calm under pressure.

Empathy, a key element of EI, enables entrepreneurs to understand and connect with their team, customers, and partners. By putting themselves in others' shoes, they can build stronger relationships and foster a collaborative work environment. Empathy also helps in identifying customer needs and providing personalized solutions, enhancing customer satisfaction and loyalty.

Social skills are the final piece of the EI puzzle. Entrepreneurs with strong social skills can effectively communicate, negotiate, and lead. They can inspire their team, resolve conflicts amicably, and create a positive company culture. These skills are not only beneficial for internal operations but also for building a strong network of external partners and investors.

2

Chapter 2: The Role of Cultural Trends in Entrepreneurship

Cultural trends play a significant role in shaping entrepreneurial ventures. They influence consumer behavior, market demand, and business strategies. Staying attuned to these trends allows entrepreneurs to anticipate changes and adapt their offerings accordingly. This agility is crucial for staying competitive in a constantly evolving market.

One major cultural trend is the rise of sustainability and environmental consciousness. Consumers are increasingly prioritizing eco-friendly products and practices. Entrepreneurs who embrace sustainable practices can attract a loyal customer base and differentiate themselves from competitors. This trend also opens up opportunities for innovative solutions that address environmental challenges.

The digital age has brought about a shift in communication and information consumption. Social media, influencer marketing, and online communities have become powerful tools for reaching and engaging customers. Entrepreneurs must leverage these platforms to build their brand, share their story, and connect with their target audience. Understanding the dynamics of digital culture is essential for effective marketing and customer relations.

Another cultural trend is the emphasis on diversity and inclusion. Businesses that value and promote diversity in their workforce and operations are more likely to succeed. A diverse team brings different perspectives, ideas, and solutions, fostering innovation and creativity. Moreover, customers and partners are drawn to companies that reflect their values and advocate for social justice.

3

Chapter 3: The Philosophy of Entrepreneurship

Entrepreneurship is not just about starting a business; it's a mindset and a way of life. It involves recognizing opportunities, taking risks, and creating value. Successful entrepreneurs have a clear vision, a strong sense of purpose, and the resilience to overcome challenges. They are driven by passion, curiosity, and a desire to make a positive impact.

At the core of entrepreneurial philosophy is the concept of value creation. Entrepreneurs identify unmet needs or problems and develop solutions that add value to people's lives. This process requires creativity, innovation, and a deep understanding of the market. It's not just about profit but also about making a difference.

Risk-taking is another fundamental aspect of entrepreneurship. Starting a business involves uncertainty, and entrepreneurs must be willing to take calculated risks. This doesn't mean being reckless, but rather carefully evaluating potential outcomes and making informed decisions. Embracing failure as a learning opportunity is also crucial for growth and success.

Resilience and perseverance are vital qualities for entrepreneurs. The journey is often fraught with obstacles and setbacks. Successful entrepreneurs maintain a positive attitude, learn from their experiences, and keep pushing forward. They are adaptable, resourceful, and committed to their vision, no matter the challenges they face.

4

Chapter 4: Emotional Intelligence in Leadership

Effective leadership is rooted in emotional intelligence. Leaders with high EI can inspire and motivate their team, build trust, and create a positive work environment. They are self-aware, empathetic, and skilled in managing relationships. These qualities are essential for guiding a team towards a common goal and achieving success.

Self-awareness allows leaders to understand their strengths and weaknesses, as well as their impact on others. This insight helps them to lead with authenticity and integrity. By recognizing their own emotions, leaders can manage their reactions and make rational decisions, even in high-pressure situations.

Empathy is crucial for building strong relationships with team members. Leaders who understand and care about their team's needs and concerns can foster a supportive and collaborative work environment. This connection boosts morale, engagement, and productivity. Empathetic leaders are also better equipped to resolve conflicts and navigate interpersonal dynamics.

Social skills are essential for effective communication and collaboration. Leaders with strong social skills can articulate their vision, provide constructive feedback, and inspire their team. They can also build and maintain a network of external partners and stakeholders. These skills are vital for creating a cohesive and motivated team, as well as for driving organizational success.

5

Chapter 5: Adapting to Cultural Trends

Entrepreneurs must stay attuned to cultural trends to remain relevant and competitive. By understanding and adapting to these trends, they can better meet customer needs and expectations. This requires continuous learning, flexibility, and a willingness to innovate.

One way to adapt to cultural trends is by embracing diversity and inclusion. This involves creating a diverse workforce, promoting inclusive practices, and advocating for social justice. By doing so, entrepreneurs can attract a broader customer base and build a positive brand image. Diversity and inclusion also drive innovation by bringing different perspectives and ideas to the table.

Sustainability is another important trend. Entrepreneurs can adopt eco-friendly practices, such as using renewable resources, reducing waste, and minimizing their carbon footprint. This not only benefits the environment but also appeals to environmentally conscious consumers. Sustainable practices can also lead to cost savings and operational efficiencies.

Leveraging digital platforms is essential for staying connected with customers and stakeholders. Entrepreneurs must understand the dynamics of social media, influencer marketing, and online communities. By engaging with their audience through these channels, they can build their brand, share their story, and gather valuable feedback. This digital presence is crucial for staying competitive in today's market.

6

Chapter 6: Innovation and Creativity

Innovation and creativity are at the heart of entrepreneurship. Entrepreneurs must constantly seek new ideas, challenge the status quo, and find creative solutions to problems. This requires a mindset of curiosity, openness, and a willingness to take risks.

One way to foster innovation is by creating a culture that encourages experimentation and learning. This involves providing resources and support for new ideas, as well as celebrating successes and learning from failures. By creating a safe space for innovation, entrepreneurs can inspire their team to think creatively and push boundaries.

Collaboration is also key to innovation. Entrepreneurs should seek diverse perspectives and collaborate with others, both within and outside their organization. This can lead to new insights, ideas, and opportunities. By building a network of collaborators, entrepreneurs can tap into a wealth of knowledge and resources.

Another important aspect of innovation is staying attuned to market trends and customer needs. Entrepreneurs must continuously gather feedback, conduct market research, and stay informed about industry developments. This allows them to identify emerging opportunities and adapt their offerings to meet changing demands.

7

Chapter 7: Building a Strong Brand

A strong brand is essential for entrepreneurial success. It sets a business apart from competitors, builds customer loyalty, and creates a positive reputation. Building a strong brand involves understanding your target audience, defining your brand identity, and consistently delivering on your brand promise.

The first step in building a strong brand is understanding your target audience. This involves identifying their needs, preferences, and values. By gaining a deep understanding of your customers, you can tailor your products, services, and marketing efforts to meet their expectations.

Defining your brand identity is also crucial. This involves creating a clear and compelling brand message, logo, and visual elements. Your brand identity should reflect your values, mission, and unique selling proposition. It's important to maintain consistency across all touchpoints, from your website and social media to your packaging and customer interactions.

Consistency is key to building a strong brand. This means delivering on your brand promise in every interaction with customers. Whether it's providing exceptional customer service, delivering high-quality products, or maintaining ethical practices, consistency builds trust and loyalty. It's also important to stay true to your brand values, even in the face of challenges or changes in the market.

8

Chapter 8: The Power of Networking

Networking is a powerful tool for entrepreneurs. It allows them to build relationships, gain new insights, and access resources and opportunities. Effective networking involves being proactive, genuine, and strategic in building and maintaining connections.

One way to build a strong network is by attending industry events, conferences, and meetups. These gatherings provide opportunities to meet like-minded individuals, share ideas, and learn from others. It's important to approach networking with an open mind and a willingness to listen and learn.

Social media platforms, such as LinkedIn, can also be valuable for networking. Entrepreneurs can connect with professionals, join groups, and participate in discussions. By actively engaging on these platforms, they can expand their network and build their online presence.

Building genuine relationships is key to effective networking. This involves being authentic, showing interest in others, and providing value. It's important to focus on building mutually beneficial relationships, rather than just seeking personal gain. By offering support, sharing knowledge, and helping others, entrepreneurs can build a strong and supportive network.

9

Chapter 9: Financial Management

Financial management is crucial for the success of any entrepreneurial venture. It involves planning, organizing, and controlling financial resources to achieve business goals. Effective financial management ensures that a business remains solvent, profitable, and able to grow.

The first step in financial management is creating a budget. A budget helps entrepreneurs allocate resources, monitor expenses, and make informed financial decisions. It provides a roadmap for managing cash flow, forecasting revenue, and planning for future investments. By setting financial goals and tracking progress, entrepreneurs can ensure they stay on track and make adjustments as needed.

Cash flow management is another critical aspect of financial management. Entrepreneurs must monitor the inflow and outflow of cash to ensure they have enough liquidity to cover expenses and invest in growth opportunities. This involves managing accounts receivable and payable, as well as maintaining a buffer of cash reserves for emergencies.

Financial analysis and reporting are also essential for informed decision-making. Entrepreneurs should regularly review financial statements, such as the balance sheet, income statement, and cash flow statement, to assess the health of their business. This analysis helps identify trends, uncover potential issues, and make data-driven decisions. It's important to seek the advice of financial experts, such as accountants and advisors, to ensure accurate and comprehensive financial management.

10

Chapter 10: Marketing Strategies

Marketing is a key component of entrepreneurial success. It involves promoting products or services to attract and retain customers. Effective marketing strategies are essential for building brand awareness, generating leads, and driving sales. Entrepreneurs must understand their target market, develop a compelling value proposition, and leverage various marketing channels.

One important marketing strategy is content marketing. By creating valuable and relevant content, entrepreneurs can engage their audience, establish authority, and build trust. This content can take various forms, such as blog posts, videos, social media posts, and e-books. The key is to provide valuable information that addresses the needs and interests of the target audience.

Social media marketing is another powerful tool for reaching and engaging customers. Entrepreneurs can use platforms like Facebook, Instagram, Twitter, and LinkedIn to share their story, connect with their audience, and promote their products or services. Social media allows for direct interaction with customers, gathering feedback, and building a loyal community.

Search engine optimization (SEO) is essential for improving online visibility and attracting organic traffic. By optimizing their website and content for search engines, entrepreneurs can increase their chances of being found by potential customers. This involves using relevant keywords, creating high-quality content, and building backlinks. SEO is a long-term strategy that requires ongoing effort and adaptation to changing algorithms.

11

Chapter 11: Customer Relationship Management

Building and maintaining strong customer relationships is vital for entrepreneurial success. Customer relationship management (CRM) involves strategies and practices for managing interactions with customers, improving satisfaction, and fostering loyalty. A strong CRM system helps entrepreneurs understand their customers, provide personalized experiences, and address their needs effectively.

The first step in CRM is gathering and analyzing customer data. This includes information about customer preferences, behavior, and feedback. By understanding their customers, entrepreneurs can tailor their products, services, and marketing efforts to meet their needs. Data analysis also helps identify trends, segment customers, and develop targeted strategies.

Personalization is key to building strong customer relationships. Entrepreneurs should strive to provide personalized experiences, whether it's through tailored recommendations, customized offers, or personalized communication. By showing that they understand and value their customers, entrepreneurs can build trust and loyalty.

Effective communication is essential for CRM. Entrepreneurs should maintain regular and meaningful interactions with their customers through various channels, such as email, social media, and customer support. It's important to listen to customer feedback, address concerns promptly, and provide exceptional customer service. By maintaining open and honest communication, entrepreneurs can build strong and lasting relationships.

12

Chapter 12: Scaling Your Business

Scaling a business involves expanding operations, increasing revenue, and reaching new markets. It's a crucial stage for entrepreneurs who want to grow their ventures and achieve long-term success. Scaling requires careful planning, strategic investments, and a focus on efficiency and quality.

The first step in scaling is developing a growth strategy. This involves identifying opportunities for expansion, setting clear goals, and creating a roadmap for achieving them. Entrepreneurs must assess their resources, capabilities, and market conditions to determine the best approach for scaling their business. This could involve launching new products, entering new markets, or acquiring new customers.

Investing in technology and automation is essential for scaling. By leveraging technology, entrepreneurs can streamline operations, improve efficiency, and reduce costs. Automation tools can help manage repetitive tasks, such as customer relationship management, inventory management, and marketing campaigns. This allows entrepreneurs to focus on strategic activities and drive growth.

Building a strong team is crucial for scaling a business. Entrepreneurs must hire talented and dedicated employees who share their vision and values. It's important to invest in employee development, provide growth opportunities, and foster a positive work culture. A strong team can drive innovation, improve productivity, and support the business's growth.

13

Chapter 13: Navigating Challenges and Setbacks

Entrepreneurship is a journey filled with challenges and setbacks. Successful entrepreneurs are resilient and resourceful, able to navigate obstacles and turn them into opportunities. This chapter explores strategies for overcoming challenges, managing stress, and maintaining a positive mindset.

One common challenge entrepreneurs face is dealing with failure. Failure is an inevitable part of the entrepreneurial journey, but it's also a valuable learning opportunity. Entrepreneurs should view failure as a chance to gain insights, improve their strategies, and grow. By embracing failure and learning from it, they can build resilience and increase their chances of success.

Managing stress is essential for maintaining mental and physical well-being. Entrepreneurs often face high levels of stress due to the demands of running a business. It's important to prioritize self-care, practice mindfulness, and seek support from mentors, peers, or professionals. By managing stress effectively, entrepreneurs can stay focused, make better decisions, and maintain a positive outlook.

Another challenge is dealing with uncertainty and change. The business landscape is constantly evolving, and entrepreneurs must be adaptable and flexible. This involves staying informed about industry trends, being open to new ideas, and embracing innovation. By being proactive and prepared for change, entrepreneurs can navigate uncertainty and seize new opportunities.

14

Chapter 14: Ethical Entrepreneurship

Ethical entrepreneurship involves conducting business in a way that is responsible, transparent, and aligned with moral values. Entrepreneurs must consider the impact of their actions on stakeholders, society, and the environment. By prioritizing ethics, entrepreneurs can build trust, enhance their reputation, and contribute to positive social change.

One aspect of ethical entrepreneurship is ensuring fair and equitable treatment of employees. This includes providing fair wages, safe working conditions, and opportunities for growth and development. Entrepreneurs should also promote diversity and inclusion, creating a workplace where all employees feel valued and respected.

Environmental sustainability is another important consideration. Entrepreneurs should adopt eco-friendly practices, such as reducing waste, conserving resources, and minimizing their carbon footprint. By taking steps to protect the environment, they can attract environmentally conscious customers and contribute to the well-being of the planet.

Transparency and honesty are essential for building trust with customers, partners, and stakeholders. Entrepreneurs should communicate openly about their business practices, products, and services. This includes being honest about any challenges or issues they face. By being transparent, entrepreneurs can build credibility and foster long-term relationships.

15

Chapter 15: The Future of Entrepreneurship

The future of entrepreneurship is shaped by emerging trends, technologies, and societal changes. Entrepreneurs must stay informed and adaptable to thrive in a rapidly evolving landscape. This chapter explores key trends and opportunities that will shape the future of entrepreneurship.

One major trend is the rise of the digital economy. Advances in technology, such as artificial intelligence, blockchain, and the Internet of Things, are transforming industries and creating new opportunities for innovation. Entrepreneurs who leverage these technologies can develop cutting-edge solutions, improve efficiency, and create new business models.

The gig economy is another significant trend. More people are seeking flexible work arrangements and freelance opportunities. This shift presents opportunities for entrepreneurs to tap into a diverse and skilled workforce. By offering gig and remote work options, entrepreneurs can attract top talent and adapt to changing workforce dynamics.

Social entrepreneurship is gaining momentum as more entrepreneurs seek to address social and environmental challenges. Social entrepreneurs prioritize impact over profit, developing solutions that benefit society and the planet. This trend reflects a growing awareness of the importance of

CHAPTER 15: THE FUTURE OF ENTREPRENEURSHIP

sustainability and corporate responsibility.

16

Chapter 16: The Entrepreneurial Mindset

The entrepreneurial mindset is characterized by a set of attitudes, behaviors, and skills that enable individuals to identify opportunities, take risks, and create value. Developing an entrepreneurial mindset involves cultivating qualities such as curiosity, resilience, and adaptability.

Curiosity is the foundation of the entrepreneurial mindset. Entrepreneurs are driven by a desire to learn, explore, and understand the world around them. This curiosity fuels creativity and innovation, enabling entrepreneurs to identify new opportunities and develop novel solutions.

Resilience is another essential quality. The entrepreneurial journey is filled with challenges and setbacks, and entrepreneurs must be able to bounce back from failures and keep moving forward. Resilience involves maintaining a positive attitude, learning from experiences, and staying committed to one's goals.

Adaptability is crucial in a constantly changing business environment. Entrepreneurs must be flexible and open to new ideas, willing to pivot their strategies as needed. This adaptability allows them to stay relevant, seize opportunities, and navigate uncertainty.

17

Chapter 17: The Legacy of Entrepreneurship

The legacy of entrepreneurship extends beyond individual success and financial gain. Entrepreneurs have the power to create lasting impact, shape industries, and inspire future generations. This chapter explores the broader contributions of entrepreneurship and the importance of leaving a positive legacy.

One way entrepreneurs can leave a lasting impact is by fostering innovation. By developing new products, services, and technologies, entrepreneurs drive progress and improve the quality of life. Their contributions can have far-reaching effects, transforming industries and benefiting society as a whole.

Entrepreneurs also play a vital role in job creation. By starting and growing businesses, they provide employment opportunities and contribute to economic growth. This not only improves the livelihoods of their employees but also stimulates local economies and strengthens communities.

Mentorship and support for future entrepreneurs are essential components of a lasting legacy. Successful entrepreneurs can share their knowledge, experience, and resources with aspiring entrepreneurs, helping them navigate challenges and achieve their goals. By giving back to the entrepreneurial community, they can inspire and empower the next generation of innovators.

Finally, entrepreneurs can leave a positive legacy by advocating for social and environmental causes. By using their influence and resources to support initiatives that align with their values, they can drive positive change and make a meaningful impact. Whether it's through philanthropy, advocacy, or sustainable business practices, entrepreneurs have the power to create a better world.

The Mind of the Market: Emotional Intelligence, Cultural Trends, and the Philosophy of Entrepreneurship

Dive into the intricate dance between emotions, culture, and entrepreneurial spirit in "The Mind of the Market." This book explores the vital role of Emotional Intelligence (EI) in entrepreneurship, revealing how understanding and managing emotions can lead to better leadership, stronger relationships, and more informed decisions.

Embrace the cultural trends that shape today's business landscape, from sustainability and digital transformation to diversity and inclusion. Learn how to adapt and thrive in a constantly evolving market by staying attuned to these trends.

Discover the philosophy of entrepreneurship—a mindset that goes beyond just starting a business. Understand the importance of value creation, risk-taking, and resilience in building a successful venture.

With insights on innovation, financial management, marketing strategies, and ethical practices, this book is a comprehensive guide for aspiring and seasoned entrepreneurs alike. Whether you're looking to scale your business, build strong customer relationships, or leave a positive legacy, "The Mind of the Market" offers the wisdom and tools to succeed in the dynamic world of entrepreneurship.

www.ingramcontent.com/pod-product-compliance
Lightning Source LLC
LaVergne TN
LVHW020741090526
838202LV00057BA/6159